One morning in 1953, I received a telephone call from my agent Charles Bloch. He wanted me to go over to Paramount Studios and cover the still-session of a young actress who had made a big impression on the studio brass in the William Wyler film, Roman Holiday.

Growing up in LA, my early photographic assignments were often with young starlets. Or, if they were more up-market, they were called young "actresses". They were usually very nice and sincere young hopefuls, but I dreamed of more important assignments at the time. After all, hadn't I started my photographic turn with Harper's Bazaar? Charles had to keep reminding me that it was these assignments, usually for fan magazines, that paid the rent and kept me in fresh film and darkroom gear.

I arrived at the Paramount Stills Gallery and got talking with the head portrait photographer, Bud Fraker, while we waited for our subject, when out of the dressing room floated a vision in voile. Bud caught my look of admiration, and almost had to help me close my open mouth. "She's something isn't she?" he said, looking toward this beauty and then back to me. He took his position behind the huge 8x10 studio portrait camera, leaving me to sort out my own equipment.

I always watched how other photographers lit their subjects, for I had originally apprenticed in a portrait studio, but my eye keep drifting back to that face... I couldn't put my finger on what it was, but she had something special. It was only after Bud had finished shooting her in that dress, that anyone thought to introduce me. I heard someone say…

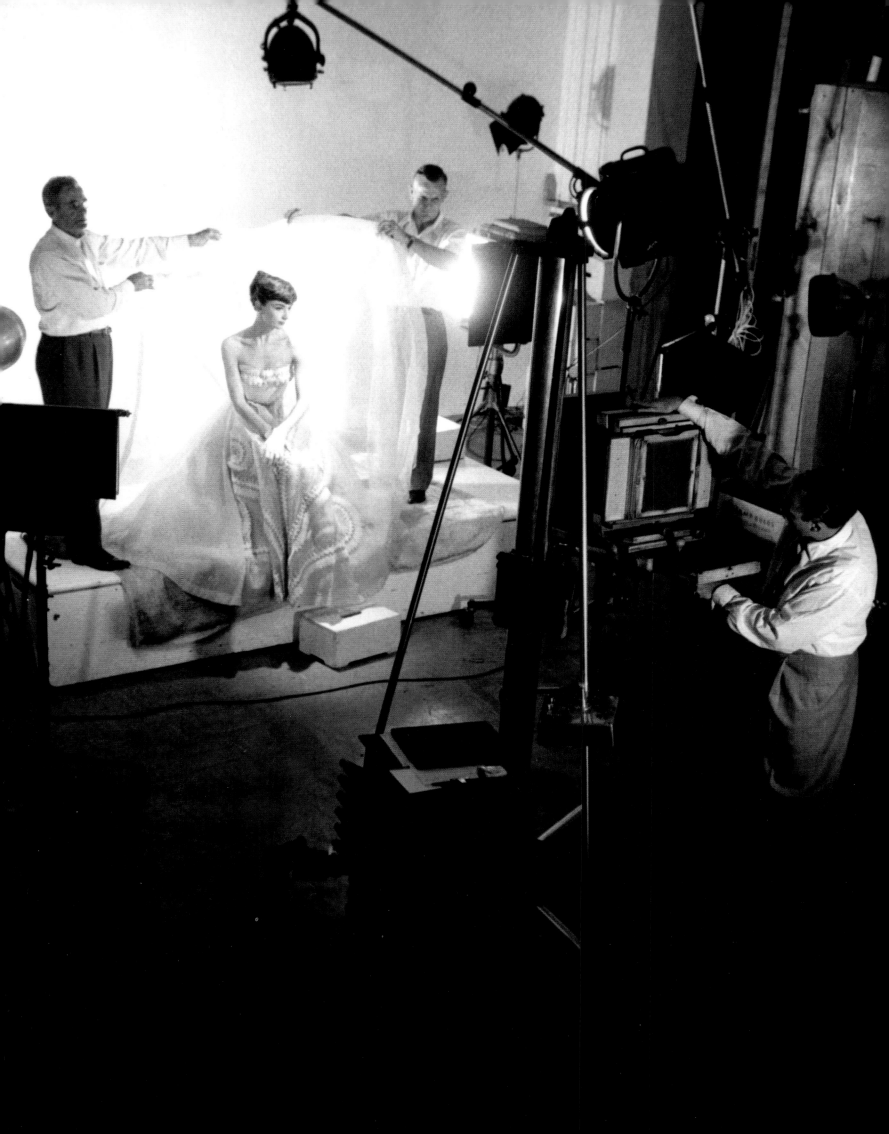

"Bob.

This is Audrey Hepburn."

Below Bud Fraker adjusting Audrey's arm... the clothes-pins in the back helped remove the wrinkles on the front of her sweater.

Opposite Audrey gossiping with Edith Head. Edith had designed Audrey's costumes for Roman Holiday, the film which established Hepburn firmly in the Hollywood firmament.

And she took my hand and dazzled me with a smile that god had designed to melt mortal men's hearts... and spoke with a voice filled with smiles. No little starlet this!

Needless to say, my early apathy when given the assignment had turned to real enthusiasm. As the publicity people trotted in some of their personalities to meet Audrey, I was amazed at how graciously, and with what ease, she presented herself to them. Later, after seeing Roman Holiday, I realised that this 24-year-old really was the princess she portrays.

The session went on for most of the day, with a quick bite to
eat that the studio provided from their commissary. Bud
Fraker seemed tireless, I could see how enthusiastic he was
about his subject... But if Bud seemed tireless, then Audrey
never stopped either, out of one dress and into another. Studio
hairdressers, wardrobe ladies and makeup were on stand-by.
This was a big production; obviously Paramount was going
all out for Miss Hepburn.

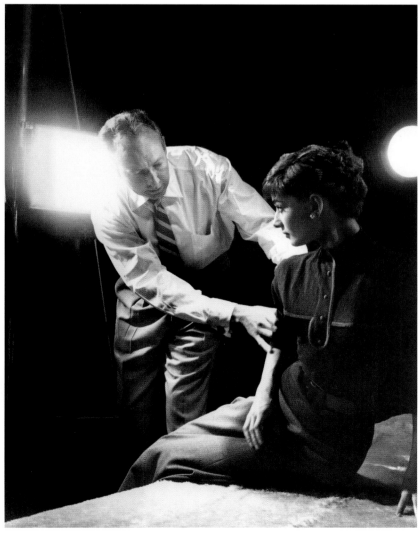

The final photograph of the day was in her own nightgown, which had a little "A" embroidered on it. Audrey didn't have to act tired, that yawn was spontaneous. However, the Paramount publicity department wasn't finished with her, and they whisked her over to the dressing room of Dean Martin and Jerry Lewis to take a few more photos.

I really don't think they were expecting the publicity department, and if they were, Jerry wasn't happy about the interruption. When he pulled this face for the photographer, Dean had to reprimand Jerry and tell him to be nice. At the time, I'm sure they would never have guessed that this young lady's career in the film world would eclipse both of theirs.

The final chore was over, and Audrey was like a child getting out of school. She went skipping down the studio street as she headed to the car that would take her back to her apartment.

After the Paramount publicity marathon was completed, I followed the studio car back to the Chapman Park Hotel on Wilshire Boulevard where Audrey was staying. I knew she must have been exhausted, however she was still game for me to come up and take a few more photographs in her room.

This is part of her character which I would observe again and again in the years that followed. She was gracious to a fault, and about as professional as anyone I've ever met.

I helped her carry up her wardrobe, and she gathered her mail at the front desk as we went by. The clothes went on the bed to be very carefully folded, but first she took sustenance from a letter from home.

Audrey had been touring with the stage play Gigi, and it was playing in Los Angeles at the time. One of my favourite portraits of Audrey was taken at the end of this very full day. Surrounded by azaleas, she was wearing her striped blouse from the play.

Paramount Studios, 1953

"Ip"

I had just returned from an assignment in the Far East when MGM telephoned to ask if I would like to cover their film Green Mansions. Two years earlier they had assigned me to photograph the film Raintree County, with Elizabeth Taylor and Montgomery Clift. Due to the amazing amount of space I got for them in the world press, I'd been busy with their assignments ever since.

The idea of a "home" assignment was very appealing. I remembered reading William Henry Hudson's romantic novel when I was very young, and thought it should be interesting as a film. The best news of all was that Audrey was to be the star, and of course I immediately said yes.

It had been nearly five years since I first met Audrey, and since then our separate careers had both taken off.

In 1954, Warner Brothers Studios had hired me to cover A Star Is Born, with Judy Garland, to get space for them in the national magazines. This was a fantastic opportunity for me, and began a chain reaction that really set the course of my life. Also, the Director Otto Preminger had taken me under his wing, and I covered his productions of Carmen Jones, The Man with the Golden Arm and Saint Audrey had now become a truly major star, having won an Academy Award for Roman Holiday and a TONY for her Broadway play, Ondine. She had married her co-star, Mel Ferrer, and today all her films are treasured. She had made Sabrina, War and Peace, Funny Face, Love in the Afternoon and The Nun's Story. The latter saw her with another Academy Award nomination, and in the process confirmed her standing as the most bankable of all actresses.

I went over to the MGM set of Green Mansions, to see if I could garner any ideas for the magazines. When I arrived on the sound stage, the technicians were in the process of creating a tropical rain forest. Cranes were hauling in massive trees and exotic plants, it was fantastic to watch. And weeks later when the production began, the thrill of walking into the cool of a tropical forest from out of the California sun will stay with me for the rest of my life.

I had heard that, years before, MGM had assigned Vincente Minelli to direct the film, and apparently he had even travelled to Venezuela to see about shooting the film on location. MGM shelved the project as too expensive until Audrey and her husband Mel Ferrer (who would now direct it) came along to rejuvenate it.

Audrey saw me standing there and greeted me as enthusiastically as if I were an old friend, and immediately introduced me to Mel. It was as if we had been working together just a few months before. The dazzling smile that warms one inside was at full power. It's an amazing ability to be able to create that feeling in others, and I could easily see why all of her leading men fell in love with her.

I was given a copy of the script, and in passing Audrey mentioned about the pet deer she was living with. Mel wanted to create the idea that the deer followed her wherever she went. If the character of Rima (that Audrey was to play) was a forest spirit, a part of nature itself, then the animals must feel that she was part of their world and posed absolutely no threat.

The animal trainers had told them that the only way to do this was to take a very young fawn and live with it. To establish a bond, so that it would get used to Audrey's touch and smell. Here was my perfect picture story and I made arrangements to meet Audrey at the house that she and Mel were renting in Beverly Hills during the making of this film.

*Audrey had already had the deer with her for several weeks,
and it had become a part of the family... well, almost.
Audrey's Yorkshire, "Famous", would give it a wide berth
(it was much bigger than he was!). He was very jealous,
like the first child being pushed off centre stage when a new
baby arrives.*

*Actually it was an amazing sight to see Audrey with the deer.
Ip would come right up and lie down next to her when she
was having a nap, and fall asleep with her. Since Audrey was
the only one allowed to feed it, I'm sure it felt that Audrey
was its mother. It was no small thing, this close bonding, and
I attributed it to Audrey's inner calm. They were literally in
touch, something I had never seen before between a human
being and a forest animal.*

Audrey took Ip shopping in Beverly Hills, and what a sensation she created. Beverly Hills habitués are fairly blasé about what they see, but Audrey being followed around town by this lovely creature stopped everyone in their tracks.

First stop was Gelson's supermarket, where a friendly butcher tried to tempt Ip with a bit of parsley. But I guess since it didn't come from her "mother", she was a bit suspicious.

What was interesting to me at the time was that, while people were naturally curious about this wonderful animal, not one person crowded in and tried to pet it or ask Audrey about it. I can't explain why that was. Could it have been respect for her privacy?

I had observed this on set of the films I worked on with her as well. None of the crew would come over for a chat while she was sitting studying her script, as they might with the other actors. Audrey was always gracious and warm and caring, yet somehow people had a special respect for her personal space; something I know many actors today would more than envy.

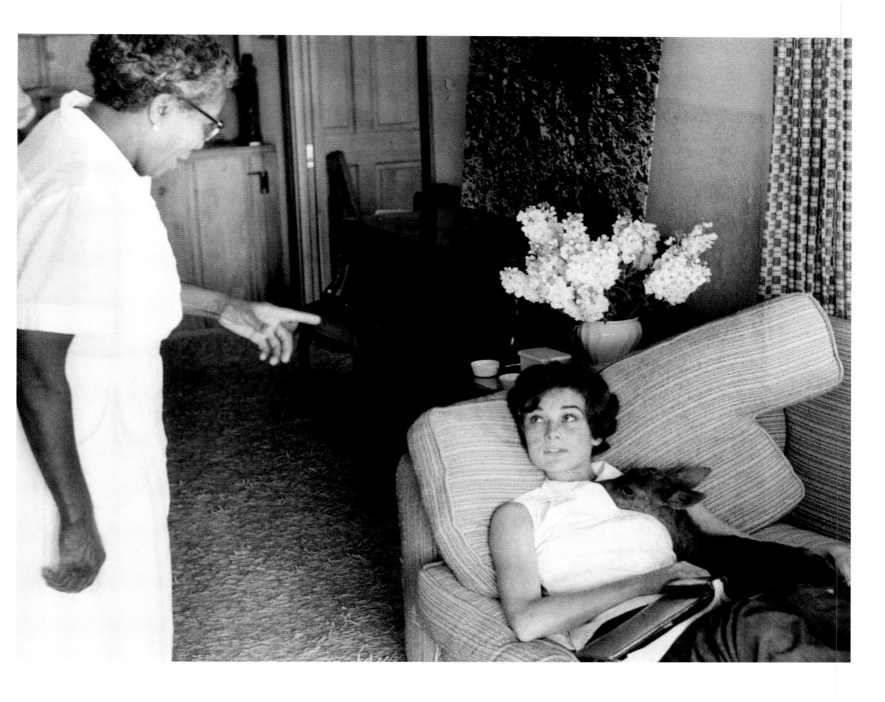

A bit of clothes shopping at Jax's Beverley Hills, where the owner Jack Hansen seems oblivious that the fawn deer is anything unusual. The last stop was at *Will Wright's Ice Cream Parlour* with her secretary and 'Famous.' Even 'Ip' would get a little treat, as *Audrey* brought his bottle along just in case.

While Audrey's maid had been told about the little deer she could not believe her eyes seeing the little deer sleeping with Audrey so calmly. She was shaking her head and just kept smiling – a sight to behold!

Working on a film set as a photographer can be quite exciting; watching the director and the actors and the action involved. However the lighting and other preparations can take hours, and one camera angle is often repeated over and over again.

Some directors I've worked with will make the actors do the same shot dozens of times until they are literally on their knees. Days can be spent covering all the angles of just one scene. After a while this can get to you. Spending one's life closed up on a dusty stage, out of the light and fresh air, can grow tiresome and frustrating.

The set of Green Mansions, however, had other perks. Here was a tropical garden populated with exotic plants, birds and animals, all created by the magicians that MGM had hired to fulfill the art director's visual fantasies. The smell of fresh earth and trees was a tranquil oasis in the concrete jungle of the MGM sound stages.

It was a remarkable set; one would turn a corner and find Audrey Hepburn hidden in the leaves... The tedium was not too hard to take.

turn a corner and find Audrey Hepburn hidden in the leaves…

I had never met Mel Ferrer before but knew his work as an actor, and I believe this was his first time out directing a film. He was naturally feeling his way, and worked hard at creating the images he had in mind.

I was impressed that, during the time I worked on the set, I never heard Audrey suggest that maybe the scene (the way Mel was setting it up) might be played differently.

Audrey had worked with some of the best directors in the business, yet there was never an argument or a complaint to Mel, just trust and loyalty, and Audrey giving everything she had to make the scenes work.

There was a lovely contact between *Audrey* and *Mel* on the set. Not as a director and his star, but of a loving couple who cared for each other. These were some of the moments I felt it was important to record.

In the film, Audrey played the part of Rima, a forest creature. I felt she should have a rather mystic quality, and I tried to capture this in my photographs.

The part really suited Audrey, dressed in the wispy costume designed by Dorothy Jeakins. At times she just seemed to merge into the trees, and almost disappear.

Green Mansions, 1958

Tony Perkins plays a young man fleeing into the Brazilian rain forest, escaping from a civil war and a hostile Indian tribe. *As he runs deeper into the trees, away from his pursuers, he knows somehow that he is being watched.*

He feels haunted by what he has seen in the city, and now hunted by the natives. He runs until he can go no further.

Falling fast asleep where he has collapsed, he wakes with amazement to see a lovely young woman kneeling near him. Surely she can't be real? The vision doesn't speak but holds out her hand to touch him... and so begins the film's love story.

Below Audrey and Tony enjoy a joke
with their co-star Lee J Cobb.

Tony Perkins kept his eye on Audrey. If he saw her sitting off the
set, maybe looking a little sad, he would jump in, shaking her
chair until he had her laughing. Getting her a cup of tea, telling
her a joke, anything that would perk up her spirits.

They had a really good relationship, and he brought out a facet
of Audrey's personality that I had never seen before. At times
they acted like two young kids. I think he was Audrey's tonic on
this film.

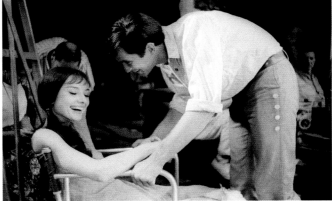

As I noted before, Audrey and Tony had a really good relationship on this film.

Tony was easy-going. I had worked with him on a couple of films previously and he had a gentle personality, ever smiling without a lot of ego to deal with. A photographer's delight.

He seemed like a brother to Audrey, and watched over her. It was lovely to see them together.

Below Maurice Chevalier comes nose-to-nose with Ip.

Right Audrey alone with her thoughts in the MGM-created rain forest.

Visitors on this set were kept to a minimum, mainly to protect the animals, but there were exceptions.

One very special guest was Marie Louise Habets (above), the real Sister Luke, whom Audrey portrayed in The Nun's Story. This may be the only existing photograph of them together. She came with Katherine Hulme, who wrote the book.

Audrey's Yorkie, Famous, was noticeably jealous of the attention that was being given to Ip, his nemesis! You can see Famous peeking out from behind the lamp as the deer gets centre stage.

He fussed so much that Audrey would make a point to take him out of the dressing room and hold him close whenever she could.

*Audrey had a calm about her that I feel the animals could sense.
I found that some of them often responded better to her than to
their handlers. You can see this with the fragile little South
American monkey. Audrey could easily take its hand in hers. Of
course to Ip, Audrey was her mother. The fawn was often startled
by all the movie equipment that was noisily trundled by, and the
shouted instructions to the lighting gang, and Audrey was
always there to protect her. Note, the wooden horse used by the
camera crew as the deer's stand-in.*

A different hat, a different expression and voila! From Rima the forest nymph to a western belle! I liked and admired Audrey when I started this film, but now I had became a devoted fan and friend.

Children...

1959 was a momentous year for both Audrey and myself. For Audrey, it wasn't good. She was thrown from a horse when filming John Huston's The Unforgiven in Mexico, and was badly injured. They rushed her home by air-ambulance and she was in the hospital for six weeks. Of course, everyone was very concerned for her, as it was reported she had broken her back in the fall.

Audrey wasn't a hardy person to begin with, and this injury only magnified that. A few months later, she suffered a miscarriage and it took her some time to recover.

I went over to see Audrey as soon as she was well enough to receive visitors at home. I'd like to try and recreate the vision I had when I walked into her bedroom. Everything was white – the bed, the floors, rugs, walls, even her crisp and fresh initialed nightgown.

When she smoked, she put the ash in a little white ashtray on her white bedside table and, when she was finished, wiped the ashtray clean with a white tissue and dropped it, of course, into a white wastebasket. It was the preciseness of her character, the way she did everything.

She was the same Audrey. She had been badly hurt, but there was that smile, like a warm embrace, to greet me. When she discussed the film and how the accident had happened, she never blamed anyone, never complained about the pain she was in. (She had to wear a back brace when she had finally recovered sufficiently to be able to return and finish the film.)

She wanted to hear my news... I had met a lovely Scottish girl when flying back from New York and had married her six weeks later. She was thrilled with the news and gave me a lovely kiss and, as I left, made me promise to bring Dorothy over to meet her.

As fate would have it, Audrey and Dorothy's first babies were born almost to the day. When the babies were almost 12 months old, Audrey and Mel came over to our home so that the boys could meet. It was 1961, and we were about to work together once more on The Children's Hour, with William Wyler.

Opposite and below The great race: Sean and Christopher race around the kitchen, with Sean in the lead and emerging victorious.

Below Audrey and Dorothy hold up the two competitors after the race, but where is the laurel-leaf crown?

A few weeks later, we went over to Audrey and Mel's place to celebrate our sons' joint first birthday party.

Below Sean getting his first taste of cake. Audrey and Mel open their mouths to demonstrate, something that everyone seems to do when feeding their children. It was a lovely day for the proud parents.

Right Audrey and Mel present our Christopher with his first birthday cake. Dorothy and her mother, Jean Quigley, just behind them are beaming with pleasure.

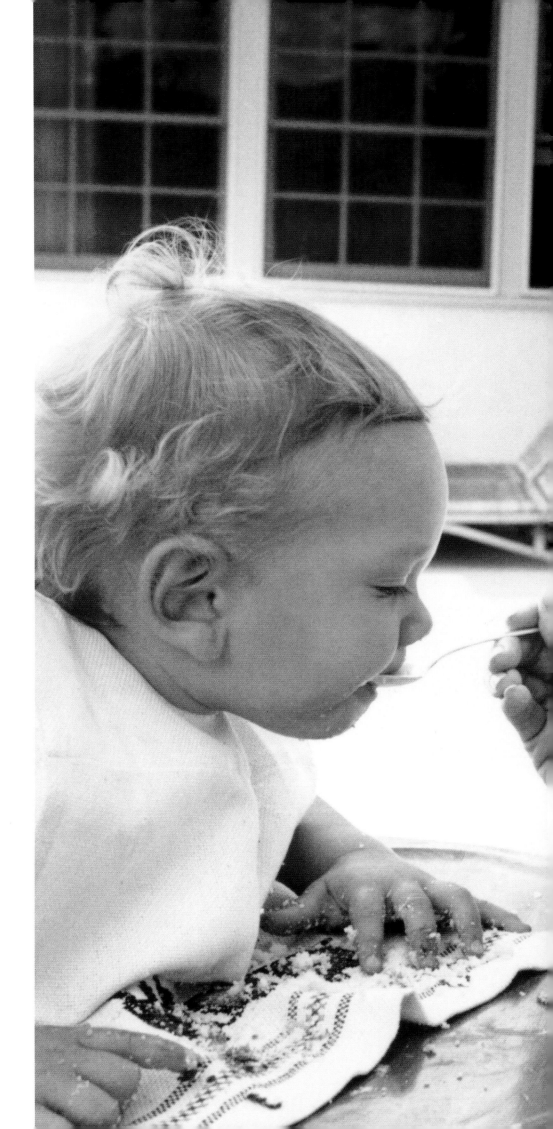

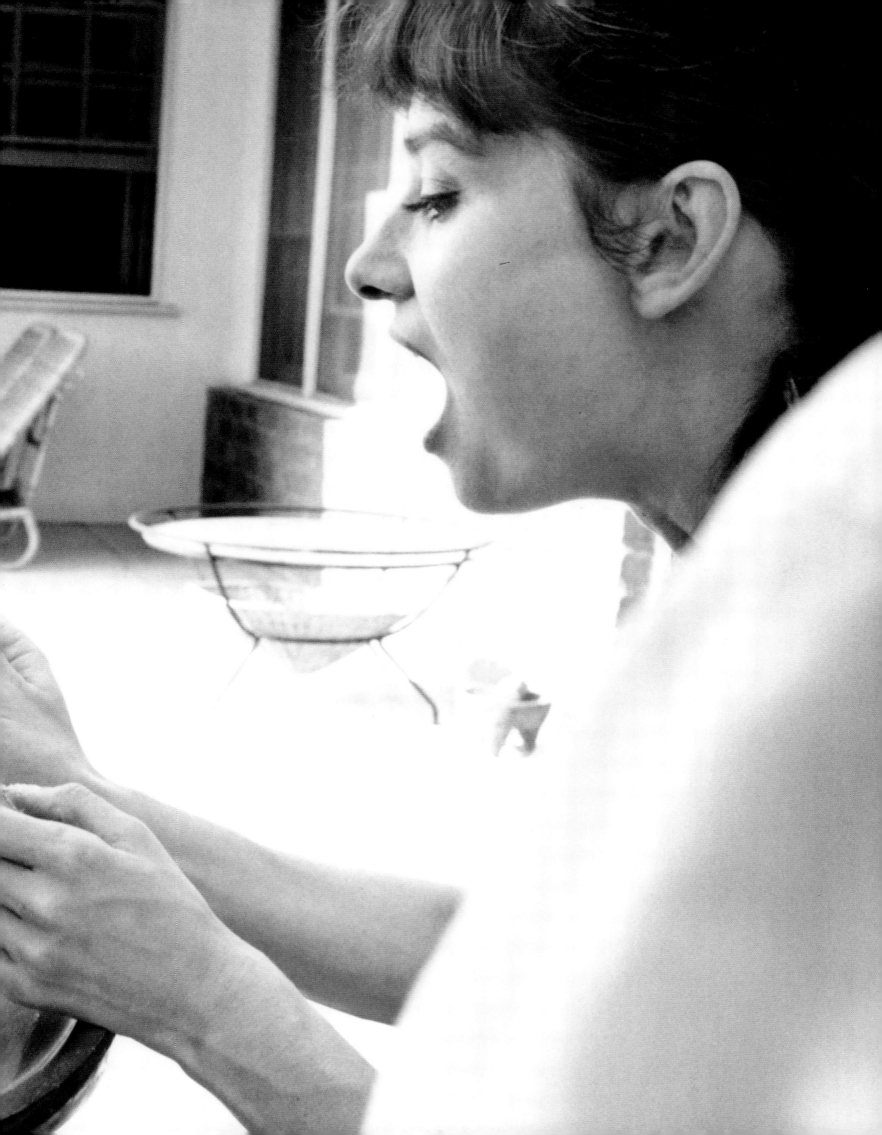

The Children's Hour was a remake of an earlier film by
William Wyler, and it was a fairly downbeat film to work on
every day. One ray of sunshine came when Audrey brought
Sean to her studio dressing room, and Jim Garner and Shirley
MacLaine, Audrey's co-stars in the film, both enjoyed the
break and had fun watching Audrey play a game with Sean.

Right Shirley enjoys playing auntie to
Sean, as Audrey looks on with pride.
Goldwyn Studios, Hollywood, 1961.

. . . *and*

The Children's Hour

The Lillian Hellman play, The Children's Hour, was basically about a child's lie that implicated two women teachers in a romance that didn't exist and ruined both of their lives.

Shirley MacLaine plays the teacher who is so distraught that, in the face of a future without her own self-respect, kills herself. Audrey plays the other teacher, who not only loses her friend, but her real romantic interest, played by James Garner.

Shooting on this film was downbeat and depressing, but was made even more grim by Wyler's directorial style. I wrote earlier about those directors who can take all week to cover the angles of just one scene. I think Wyler must have invented that approach.

Below In a scene from the film, Audrey puts her hand over Garner's mouth to stop him from saying what she knows he's thinking.

Overleaf Shirley MacLaine and Audrey Hepburn try, without success, to ply director William Wyler (in chair) using all of their female charms. Wyler was a brick wall, and steadfast with the direction of the story.

The days wound on with the same lines being repeated over and over. Wyler was never one to give directions. When I was working with Gary Cooper on another film he told me that he was mystified as to what Wyler was looking for. Gary simply had to walk down a flight of stairs and get into a stagecoach. He did it dozens of times, each time seemingly the same. Wyler would never tell him what he wanted, or what the difference was when he finally called for a print.

Keeping the dialogue fresh when it is repeated so often is difficult for any actor, and everybody seems to have their own way of dealing with the problem. I felt Audrey kept pushing herself deeper into the character, even in the rehearsals, looking for something to play on.

Other times she would just disappear, and when I went looking I would find her hidden away in an unlit part of the set. She needed to get away from all the distractions, and prepare herself to face the scene again. I would just quietly take the photograph and move away, and she pretended not to notice.

This daily grind went on and on. I returned to the set after a week, and Audrey told me that they were still on the same scene that I had covered when I left. It was not in Audrey's character to ever complain, but the emotional content of the script and the slow pace was taking its toll on everyone.

This was when Jim Garner was at his best. He had an off-the-wall humour, and when things got especially grim, he would say something funny to break everyone up, and literally save the day.

The cinematographer on the film was the dear, late Franz Planer. On a later film, Audrey told me that he had left her his Basher light (a light that sits over the motion picture camera's lens and is designed to eliminate wrinkles, and in Audrey's case, the shadows under her eyes). I mention this to show how people really cared about Audrey, that even when Franz was dying he thought of her.

I think this reveals the effect Audrey had on people. For example, I was invited recently to a TV show in honour of Audrey in Paris. Her good friend Givenchy was there, as were others who knew and had worked with her, especially at the end, when she was the UNICEF Ambassador. By the end of the evening, everyone was in tears. What more can I say?

Paris When It Sizzles, 1962

Paris When It Sizzles...

Paris When it Sizzles was Audrey's next film, and the Ferrers' rented a lovely villa just outside Paris where they could live before and during the filming. It really was more like a chateau, and had its own lake with resident swans. It gave Audrey a chance to rest up after The Children's Hour, and by the time she started rehearsals in the Boulogne Studios, she was looking terrific.

In 1962, I was working on two films in England when I received a telegram from publicity man, Martin Goldblatt. He was in Paris on Audrey's film, Paris When it Sizzles, and he said that they wanted me to cover their production. When I telephoned Martin I explained about my commitments, but he persisted and said he was sending their production breakdown. If there was any way I could shoot on their film, he told me, they would take as much time as I had.

I needed no urging to try and work something out, and when I spoke to my producers about the timing I discovered that there was to be a delay in starting the second film. What's more, they felt it wasn't necessary for me to cover it entirely... what a wonderful break! So with the first film completed, I moved the family to Paris.

From there I commuted to the UK and back half a dozen times while I was working on Sizzle. It was a busy but exciting time. Richard Quine, who I had always liked, was the director and Audrey's co-star was one of my favourite actors, William Holden.

From the first days on the Sizzle set, the atmosphere was charged with good humour... what a change from the Goldwyn set for Audrey! For me it was wonderful to have the opportunity of photographing these three vital people working together on a film, and having the time of their lives.

Paris in August used to be nice and quiet. Little or no traffic, less busy in restaurants and museums. If one needs to film exteriors of the city, this really makes it much less complicated than fighting the crowds who always watch when a film is being made.

I started my coverage of the film on this rooftop, perfect to establish in my photographs just where we were. The welcome from Audrey, Bill Holden and Richard Quine was terrific, and the French crew immediately started calling me "Monsieur Click-Click". With such a warm reception it made me feel very much at home.

Below Director Quine shows Bill Holden how he wants him to hold Audrey as they rehearse the scene, and Bill then tries it as Quine watches intently.

Finally Quine, delighted with the scene, as he swings Audrey around in delight.

Right Audrey giggles as she waits for her cue to enter the scene, where she first arrives to work for Holden. To her left, Dick Quine watches the action through the camera.

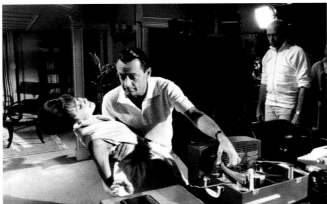

The rehearsals were great to photograph as everyone was having a great deal of fun with the scenes. I think Audrey acted as a catalyst in this, for both Bill and Dick seemed to have a little competition going for Audrey's attention.

Paris When It Sizzles, 1962

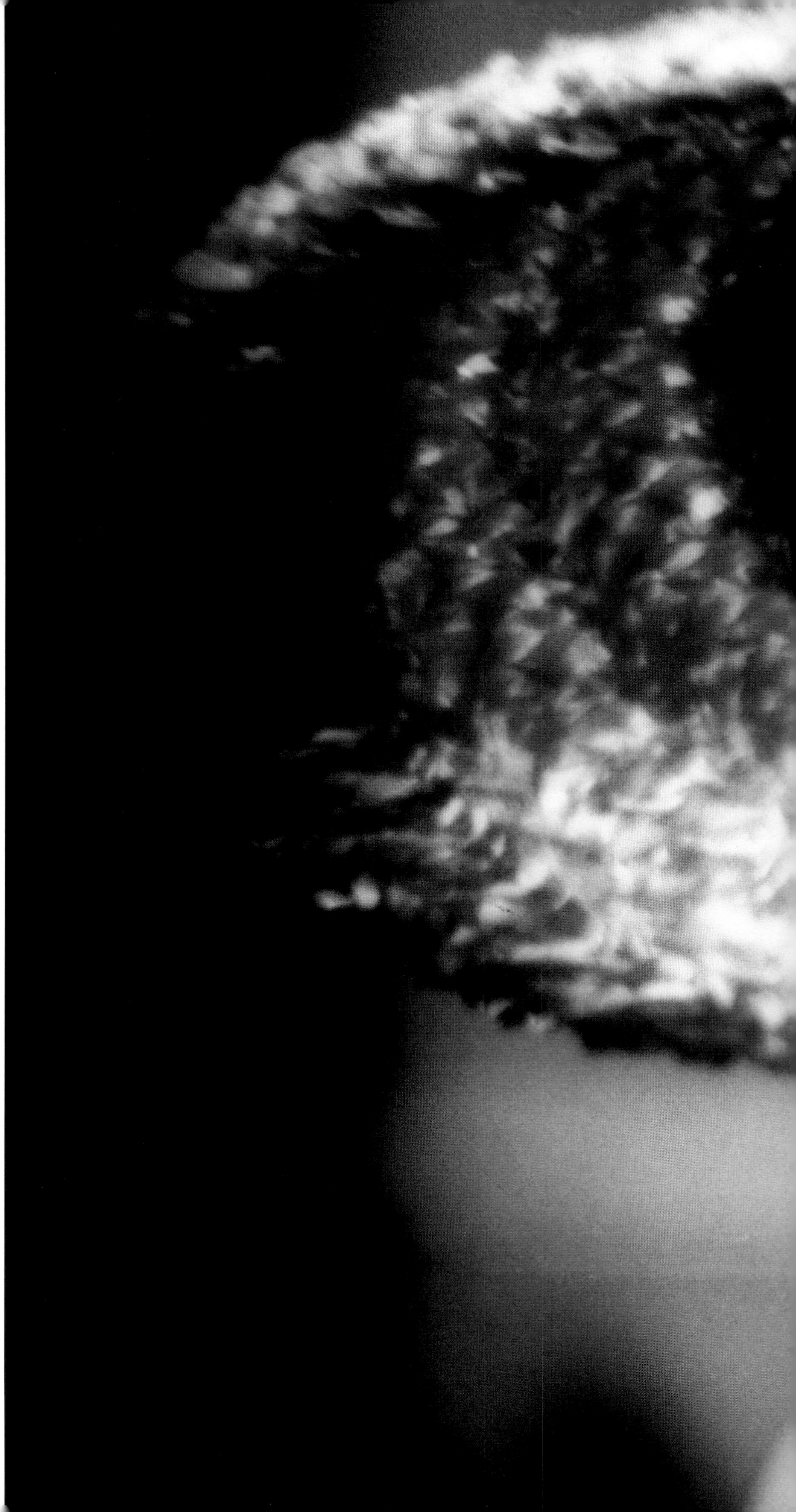

Audrey plays a secretary who is hired by William Holden to type a screenplay that he was supposed to have written, but has neglected while he's been too busy enjoying the pleasures of the Riviera. All he has is the title: The Girl Who Stole The Eiffel Tower.

Now with only three days to meet the deadline, he frantically starts making the story up. As he dictates the plot, you actually see them on screen acting out the scenes.

Then the idea is rejected and he tries something else. It also gives Audrey's character in the film a chance to shine in an array of beautiful Givenchy clothes.

Bellow and right As a photographer it was hard not to keep photographing Audrey. She could sit next to an old ladder on the set and look terrific. Wrapped in a blanket (to keep warm on the Eiffel Tower location) she just always looked amazing.

Bill Holden, trying desperately to figure out a plot for the screenplay, would dictate an idea to Audrey. And as we hear his voiceover, they would be acting out that scene.

One of the many scenarios has Holden as a movie producer trying to steal his own film... Another, Audrey's character hiding on an empty film set... Mock horror as Bill plays Dracula... Audrey as a gun moll lighting Holden's cigarette with her gun-lighter... Bill chasing a terrified Audrey around the studios office ...

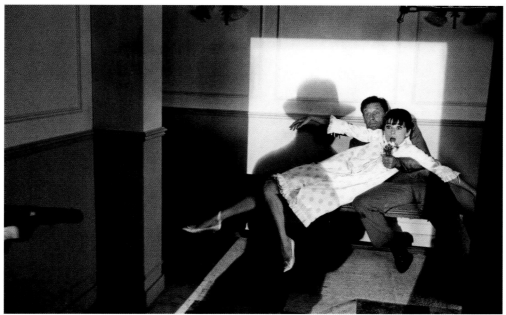

The film had so many switches on switches, that it was almost impossible to keep up with what was going on. When I had been away for a week in the UK on the other film, they would often have to re-orient me to all of the plot changes. It was mad, and one can safely say that no one had ever seen Audrey in a film quite like this before.

Left Bill chases a terrified Audrey around the studios office.

There was a great deal of chemistry flowing on the set. I was told that Bill and Audrey had a bit of a flutter when they were making Sabrina. Whether this is true or not, there was no question that Bill was in love with Audrey.

I don't think there can be any doubt that Audrey was having fun on this film. She was so effervescent and full of joy, so delicious, that I knew there were a few crew members on this film that would have liked to just scoop her up and take her home with them.

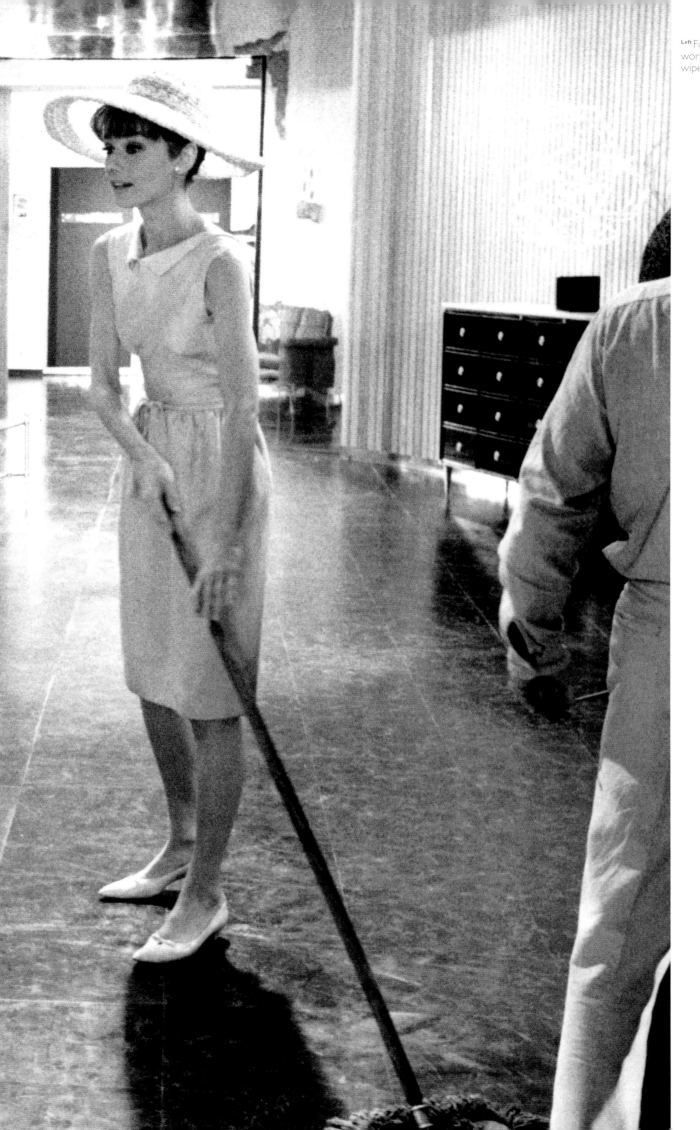

Left For fun, Audrey picks up the workman's mop after a take and wipes the floor for the next shot.

Begging like her little dog, Famous, or sitting in her dressing room with a passion flower in her hair, Audrey is just irresistible.

Below Audrey arrives at the Eiffel Tower location in medieval costume, for one of the last sequences in the film.

Opposite Even the very formal Guarde Republicaine are not able to resist Audrey's smile, as she charms them waiting for filming to begin.

Opposite Capucine visits the set and has a laugh with Audrey. Not that they are in any way competitors for Bill, but an interesting group as Capucine was once a gleam in Bill's eye as well. Screenwriter George Axelrod on the left. In the background, wearing the tie is cinematographer Charles Lang.

Below Mel Ferrer, dressed as Dr Jekel, plays a small part in the last Eiffel tower scene. Seen here with Audrey, are three of the men who loved her. Hubert Givenchy (centre), who has designed all of her clothes for the film and who was one of her greatest friends. At the left, Bill Holden dressed in his costume for the next scene.

One of the magazine layouts I made for the film was for French Vogue. With Audrey and the gorgeous Givenchy creations.

Left Audrey on the Sizzle set,
wearing Givenchy's little black dress
with Famous in the director's chair,
reading the script.

Below Audrey leaving the Boulogne
Studios, as part of the Vogue
fashion layout, wearing a little
fur jacket.

My Fair Lady had been one of Broadway's longest running and most popular stage plays ever produced and *Warner Brothers* had finally secured the film rights, but at a very high price. I think the figure given at the time was $12 million which given today's budgets seems paltry, but represented a massive risk at the time.

Audrey surely was the most bankable female actress of the era, and the plum part of Eliza Dolittle fell, rightly, to her. After *Sizzle*, she had gone right into Charade, with Cary Grant. Her schedule had been hectic and she was tired when she returned from Europe. She took three months to rest, to try and gain some weight and learn the script. Everyone knows the story line of the Lerner and Lowe musical. Eliza the little London flower girl, is transformed into an eloquent young lady by Professor Higgins (the eloqution expert) on a bet that he could pass her off as a princess at a ball.

Rex Harrison would play the part he had made his own after so many years on Broadway. There was a great supporting cast and George Cukor would direct. When *Warner Brothers* assigned me to work on the film I really felt very lucky, as I knew the world's journals would be fighting for my photographs.

For the first day of shooting the *Warner Brothers* publicity department had invited all of the world press to meet and photograph the actors for about an hour. The director George Cukor had declared that it would be a very closed set and this catered to all of the press' requests in one go.

I had not seen *Audrey* since Paris. *As* I walked behind the actors to get my first shots of the film she caught sight of me, and gave me that welcoming laser-beam smile that could curl my toes. The smile that makes anyone feel as if they were the only person she cared about in the whole world.

When My Fair Lady began shooting, I had not seen Audrey since Paris, and as I walked behind to get my first shots of the film … the press photographing the principal actors, she caught sight of me, and gave me that welcoming laser-beam smile that tended to curl my toes. The smile that makes anyone feel as if they were the only person she cared about in the whole world.

Because the film was to show Eliza being transformed, it was to be shot in sequence. Something that is never normally done, as it adds substantially to the production costs. In this case they had no choice. They must start with the scruffy and dirty Eliza.

I had noticed on the studio call sheets that Audrey's call for makeup was seven o'clock in the morning, to be ready for nine o'clock on set. Until that day however, I never really appreciated what that entailed...it meant getting up at five thirty to be into the Warner Brothers makeup department just before seven.

I was surprised to see so many people ready for the day. Frank McCoy and Dean Cole, Audrey's makeup and hairdresser, got straight right to work as soon as she swept in with her new Yorkie, "Assam", under her arm.

To make Eliza appropriately grotty, they would curl her hair tightly to make it look frizzy, coat it with Vaseline to keep it matted all day, and rub in the makeup people's dirt, known as "Fuller's Earth".

And this was the routine, every morning! After filming was completed for the day, all of this had to be undone. So, up at five thirty and home after shooting, between seven thirty and eight o'clock in the evening with luck. Not quite as glamorous a life as one might have believed film stars lead.

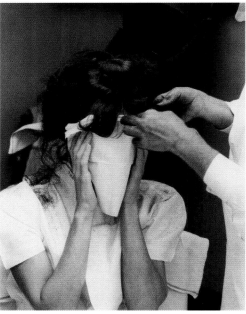

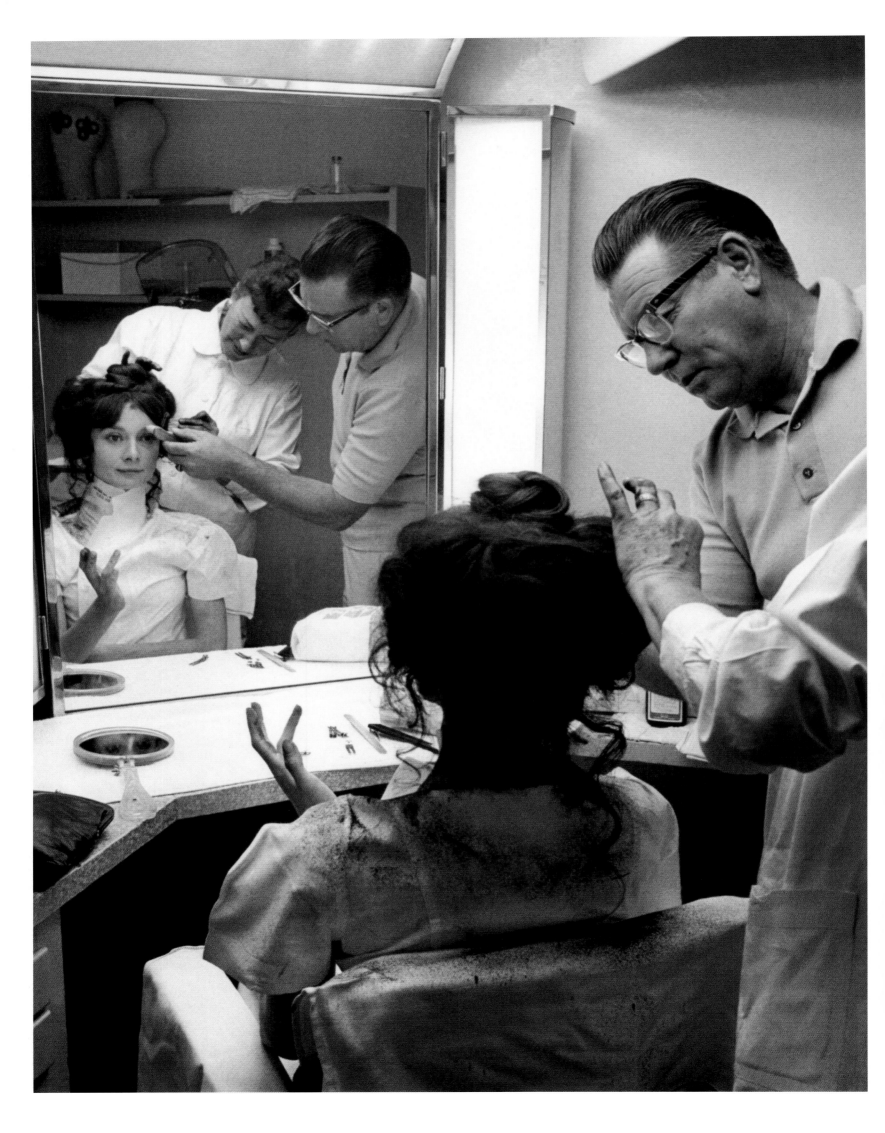

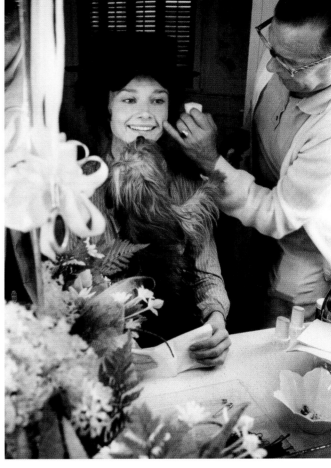

My Fair Lady, 1963

Below Audrey is hosed down by one of the crew to get her appropriately wet, since the first sequences will be filmed in the rain.

Opposite Audrey as a drenched Eliza.

My Fair Lady, 1963

Below The camera crew are sheltered from the rain effects as they shoot the close-ups, but Audrey spent the best part of the day soaked to the skin.

Below This is the scene where Eliza first meets Professor Higgins. He tells her where she lives and all about her family, just through her accent. She is mystified.

Below As Eliza listens to the Professor, she wonders if he could ever teach her to speak proppa. She might even be able to get work in a flower shop!

Overleaf Audrey singing to the playback before filming the luverly musical sequence. On the left, Rudi Friml Jr watches closely as she lip-synchs to the pre-recorded playback. Audrey told me that after she had recorded the numbers, Warner Brothers had decided her voice wasn't strong enough. Marnie Nixon did the final vocals.

"Oh wouldn't it be luverly..." It was a charming musical
sequence, and it was easy to see that Audrey was really
enjoying herself.

Overleaf After getting out of makeup, Audrey bicycles back to the sound stage to discuss the next days filming with Cukor. The director was still going over in his mind what he had shot that day.

My Fair Lady, 1963

Below Cukor was unrelenting, demanding something more in Audrey's performance.

Bottom Higgins (Rex Harrison) tempts Eliza to stay, when she threatens to leave.

Right Eliza timidly arrives at Professor Higgins' house, hoping to be able to learn to speak like a lady.

Professor Higgins instructs his housekeeper (Mona Washbourne) to "clean this Eliza creature up". He's decided to let her stay and teach her how to speak, because of a bet he had made that he could make her into a lady.

Eliza has no idea that the sweet-smelling bath salts are for her. Then the penny drops. She protests that "I'm a good girl!", but to no avail. Mona bars the door... and the fun begins.

"But I'm a good girl!!"

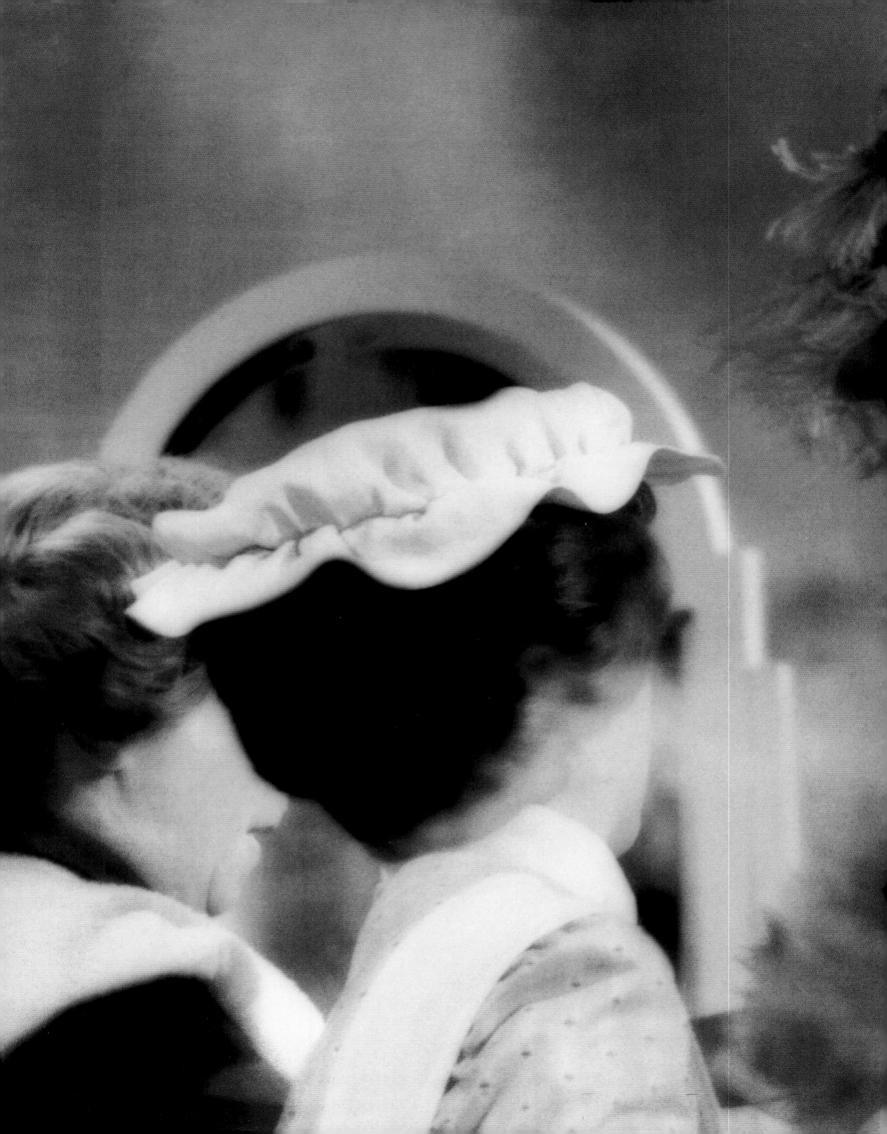

My Fair Lady, 1963

My Fair Lady, 1963

In Eliza's mind she sees the diabolical Professor Higgins, who causes her such torture, lined up before a firing squad. As she sings "Just You Wait 'Enry Higgins, Just You Wait", they shoot him, and she stands triumphantly over his body.

A scene Audrey played with such gusto that when the number was finished everybody on the set broke up laughing, she had performed it with such a fiendish delight!

When the scene where Professor Higgins faces the firing squad was over, Audrey roared with laughter, for she was having so much fun in the role.

For Eliza, however, there was no such fun in her future, as Higgins kept bringing out one torturous machine after another to test her pronunciation, and her resolve.

My Fair Lady, 1963

Professor Higgins thinks it is time to trot Eliza out for a test run, and Ascot it is... Eliza looks every bit the lady, but when she starts to speak, Higgins is horrified. Freddie (Jeremy Brett) thinks her "small talk" is wonderful, and is completely smitten.

Something must be said here about the brilliant period clothes that Cecil Beaton designed for My Fair Lady. Cecil, better known for his society photographs in the UK, surpassed himself on this film, and should be better remembered as a superb costume designer.

My Fair Lady, 1963

Audrey Hepburn in the
wonderful Cecil Beaton costume
designed for the Ascot scene.

Below After lunch, Mel would walk
Audrey through the canyons of the
Warner Brothers sound stages,
back to the My Fair Lady set.

Mel Ferrer, Audrey's husband, would often come to the studio to
have lunch with Audrey away from the world of Eliza Dolittle.
There was a great deal of pressure on Cukor at this time, and
while Audrey surely could have had Mel come on the set, she was
thoughtful enough not to impose.

As Eliza recites her mantra for the thousandth time - "The rain in Spain falls mainly on the plains" - something marvelous clicks! Higgins marvels, "By God, I think she's got it!" and in a fit of excitment and delight, sweeps Eliza up and they dance across the floor, with Colonel Pickering waving them on.

The moment of truth. Finally the time comes for Eliza to go to the ball, and for Professor Higgins to see if he can pass her off as a princess and win his bet.

What the audience already knew, is that it would be Audrey Hepburn who would walk down those stairs, and she already was a princess.

My Fair Lady, 1963

My Fair Lady, 1963

My Fair Lady, 1963

At the end of filming on My Fair Lady, the crew got together and gave Audrey a gift. I've covered over 100 films and I've never known any other crew do that. What special quality did Audrey have that everyone felt touched by her grace?

I've spoken to reporters who have interviewed her several times. They all felt as if they were her friends and yet, when pushed, none could really say that they really knew her.

When President Kennedy was assassinated, I learned about it when I called the studio to confirm the following day's shooting schedule. The assistant director told me of the tragedy, and then added, "Audrey asked the crew to stop and give a silent prayer," and it had touched everyone coming from her.

I'll wager there is not a single one of those crewmen alive today that isn't able to recall that moment vividly.

I hope these images of this vital, loving lady will be a reminder of someone special that has passed our way, and in the process touched each one of those who knew her.

Two For The Road

Walking down the road during a camera rehearsal, Audrey Hepburn and Albert Finney had an animated conversation. In fact in the few days that I spent on the film, I don't remember that they ever stopped talking.

Finny was showing Audrey his passport, and as she looked at his photograph, she was giggling. She told him that he should have "gotten Bob" to take the photo. There was always a happy banter going on between them. Albi often went into his very good Humprey Bogart imitation to make Audrey smile, since she worked with him on Sabrina.

Stanley Donen directed this interesting film that traces the lives and loves of a married couple, played by Hepburn and Finney, over many years as they auto through France on their holiday.

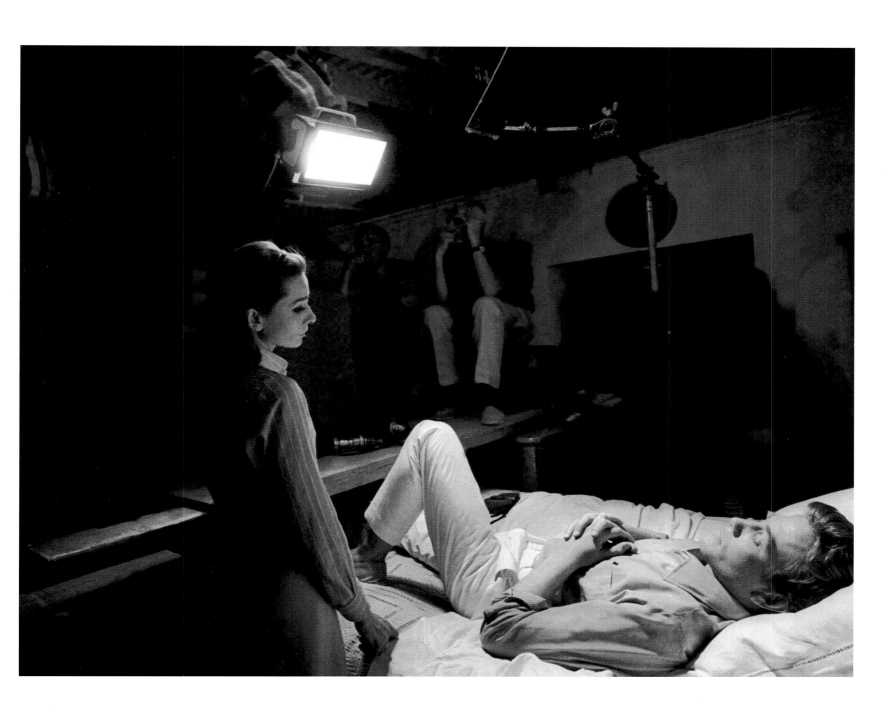

My time with *Audrey* on Two for the Road was all too short as
I had another assignment in London. *We would see each other
on a set, there would be a phone call and Christmas cards, but
our paths no longer crossed as they once did.*

*We did meet again briefly in Rome, where I met Sean again
after so many years had past, and marvelled how he had
grown, not remembering that our boys were growing as well.
When our Catherine was born, Audrey sent a card with a little
gift to Dorothy telling her how clever she was, after having had
three boys.*

*Audrey went on to serve as the UNICEF Ambassador for years,
and pushed herself physically too far. Appalled at what she had
seen with the state of little children in the many countries she
visited, she passed out of our lives in 1993. She left those who
came into contact with her better for having known her. I miss
her to this day.*

Audrey Hepburn
May 4, 1929-Jan 20, 1993

Audrey was the UNICEF Special
Ambassador for their Childrens'
Fund for five years, from 1987 to
1992, the year before she died.
She could have chosen to stay at
home in Switzerland, but knew
that her presence in these blighted
countries she visited would bring
more public awareness of the
desperate plight of the children.
Even when she knew she wasn't
well, she continued her fight for the
children. Some say that she literally
sacrificed her life for this cause.

Remember her love and
courage and give to the UNICEF
Childrens' Fund.